DATE DUE

JOE BIDEN

By Nicole Iorio

Please visit our web site at **www.garethstevens.com.**
For a free color catalog describing our list of high-quality books,
call 1-800-542-2595 (USA) or 1-800-387-3178 (Canada). Our fax: 1-877-542-2596

Library of Congress Cataloging-in-Publication Data
Iorio, Nicole.
Joe Biden / by Nicole Iorio.
p. cm. — (People we should know)
Includes bibliographical references and index.
ISBN-10: 1-4339-1949-4 ISBN-13: 978-1-4339-1949-7 (lib. bdg.)
ISBN-10: 1-4339-2148-0 ISBN-13: 978-1-4339-2148-3 (soft cover)
1. Biden, Joseph R.—Juvenile literature. 2. Vice presidents—United States—Biography—Juvenile literature. 3. Legislators—United States—Biography—Juvenile literature. 4. United States. Senate—Biography—Juvenile literature. I. Title.
E840.8.B54I67 2010
973.932092—dc22 [B] 2009003769

This edition first published in 2010 by
Gareth Stevens Publishing
A Weekly Reader® Company
1 Reader's Digest Road
Pleasantville, NY 10570-7000 USA

Executive Managing Editor: Lisa M. Herrington
Senior Editor: Brian Fitzgerald
Senior Designer: Keith Plechaty

Produced by Editorial Directions, Inc.

Art Direction and Page Production: Kathleen Petelinsek, The Design Lab

Picture credits
Cover and title page: William Thomas Cain/Getty Images; p. 5: AP Photo/Rich Schultz; p. 7: Vespasian/Alamy; p. 8: Chip Somodevilla/Getty Images; p. 9: AP Photo/Jeff Roberson; p. 11: AP Photo/Ron Edmonds; p. 12: Jewel Samad/AFP/Getty Images; p. 13: Yearbook Library; p. 14: Andre Jenny/Alamy; p. 17: Bob Adelman/Corbis; p. 18: Brendan Smialowski/epa/Corbis; p. 20, 24: AP Photo; p. 23: AP Photo/Henry Griffin; p. 27: Timothy A. Clary/AFP/Getty Images; p. 29: Bill Ballenberg//Time Life Pictures/Getty Images; p. 30: Mark Wilson/Getty Images; p. 31: Steve Liss//Time Life Pictures/Getty Images; p. 32, 35: Terry Ashe//Time Life Pictures/Getty Images; p. 36: AP Photo/Scott Applewhite; p. 39: Paul J. Richards/AFP/Getty Images; p. 40: AP Photo/Paul Sancya; p. 41: AP Photo/Rick Wilking, Pool; p. 43: AP Photo/Alex Brandon

Printed in the United States of America

1 2 3 4 5 6 7 8 9 14 13 12 11 10 09

Words in the glossary appear in **bold** type the first time they are used in the text.

Going Home

On Labor Day in 2008, Joe Biden had a cookout at his childhood home in Scranton, Pennsylvania. He hadn't lived there in more than 50 years. But he was at ease with everyone at the small gathering. The U.S. **senator** promised not to talk much about politics. Instead, he shared memories of growing up in Scranton. This was more than just a friendly visit, though. Biden had recently become his party's nominee for vice president. It was his first solo **campaign** stop in his new role.

Biden shakes hands in his hometown of Scranton on Labor Day in 2008.

His Old Neighborhood

Biden entered the gray house with black shutters at 2446 North Washington Avenue. He went up to the attic to see his childhood bedroom. The Kearns family, the home's current residents, asked Biden to write on the same wall on which he had once scribbled. On this visit, he wrote, "I am home." Biden had come back to Scranton's Green Ridge neighborhood to talk about the future of the United States.

Fast Fact

Joe Biden was often called Joey as a boy. Joey and his family lived with his grandparents for several years to save money.

Counting on Connections

Biden recalls playing baseball and shooting hoops with friends in Scranton. As a child, he picked out candy from the corner store and watched double features at the local movie theater. Joe Biden still knows people in his old neighborhood.

Biden is a Democrat. The United States has two major political parties: the Democrats and the Republicans. When Democratic presidential **candidate** Barack Obama chose Biden as his running mate, he was counting on Biden's connections with working-class families like those in Scranton. Working-class and middle-class people earn average incomes—they're not rich and they're not poor.

Grandpop Finnegan

Joe Biden first learned about politics from his grandfather, Ambrose Finnegan. "Grandpop" would talk about politics with friends at his kitchen table on Sundays after church. They would **debate** issues and would let Joey listen in. Finnegan taught his grandson to keep his promises. He also told Joey that politicians should work for all the people, not just the rich and powerful.

This is a view of downtown Scranton, Pennsylvania, Joe Biden's hometown.

Swing Town

The **blue-collar** city of Scranton is in northeastern Pennsylvania. Scranton fell on hard times after its coal and textile industries shut down in the 1960s and 1970s. Today, many people there struggle to pay their bills but are working to revive their community.

Scranton became a battleground in the 2008 presidential race. Both Barack Obama and Republican presidential candidate Senator John McCain worked to win over voters in Scranton and cities like it across the country.

Fast Fact

When Biden is in Scranton, he visits Hank's Hoagies to eat one of Pennsylvania's most famous sandwiches. Hoagies are known elsewhere as heroes, subs, or grinders.

Speaking to Voters

Since 1972, Biden had represented Delaware in the U.S. Senate. But he never forgot about the state where he was born. In 2008, Pennsylvania's economy was bad and people were suffering. "All across Pennsylvania," he said to a crowd in a Scranton soccer stadium, "folks are trying to figure out what all this tough economic news means for them and their families." He told them that he understood their worries about their jobs, homes, and health care.

Fast Fact

Biden's 10-year-old granddaughter, Finnegan, traveled with Biden during his vice presidential campaign. She is named after Biden's grandfather, Ambrose Finnegan.

Senator John McCain makes a campaign stop in Pennsylvania.

Swing State

Some states tend to favor Democratic candidates. Other states always lean Republican. Pennsylvania does neither. It is called a swing state because it can swing toward either political party. During the 2008 election, swing states such as Pennsylvania, Ohio, and Florida got a lot of attention. John McCain and his running mate, Alaska governor Sarah Palin, made multiple campaign stops in Pennsylvania in an effort to win over the state's voters.

Joe Biden and Barack Obama appear at a rally in Springfield, Illinois.

The Winning Team

On November 4, 2008, the Obama–Biden team won the Pennsylvania vote. Later that night, Obama and Biden were declared the winners of the national election. Joey from Scranton would become the next vice president of the United States.

> "We cannot win without winning Pennsylvania."
>
> —Joe Biden, speaking to supporters in August 2008

A College Man

Joseph Robinette Biden Jr. was born on November 20, 1942, in Scranton, Pennsylvania. Joey was the first child born to Joseph Sr. and Catherine Eugenia (known as Jean).

Joey's father had a hard time finding a good job in Scranton. So the Bidens moved to Wilmington, Delaware, in 1953. Joey was 10. By then, he had a younger sister, Valerie, and a younger brother, Jimmy. The family settled in Claymont, just outside of Wilmington.

Jean Biden joins her son onstage during the 2008 campaign.

Starting Over

Joey switched from St. Paul's School in Scranton to Holy Rosary School in Claymont. The school Joey dreamed about attending, though, was the beautiful mansion he could see from his window. Archmere Academy, a private all-boys high school, was the symbol of a rewarding future.

Fast Fact

Joe Biden repeated third grade. He had missed a lot of school after having his tonsils removed.

After just a few years, the Bidens moved again. The family bought a new house in Mayfield, Delaware. Joey went to St. Helena School in seventh grade.

Today, Biden is a gifted public speaker.

Dash

As a kid, Joe's nickname was "Dash," not for his speed at sports but because of his stutter. Joe's classmates thought his stop-and-start speech sounded like Morse code. Morse code is a telegraph language that uses a series of dots and dashes to make letters.

Joe would stutter when he read aloud in class. His classmates laughed at him. To overcome his weakness, Joe memorized long passages from poetry books and said them repeatedly in front of a mirror at home. By 10th grade, he had overcome his stutter.

A Fish Out of Water

In the 1950s, Mayfield was a fast-growing community. College-educated professionals were settling their families there. Many worked at DuPont, a large chemical company based in Wilmington. Joe's father was unlike most other fathers in the area. He had never gone to college. He took the work he could get, whether cleaning furnaces or selling used cars.

Fast Fact

As a kid, Joe Biden delivered newspapers in his Mayfield neighborhood.

Joe Biden poses for his senior photo at Archmere Academy.

The First Step

Joe's father always regretted not going to college. He often reminded Joe, "You've got to be a college man." When Joe was accepted at Archmere Academy, he was on his way.

At Archmere, Joe spent time in the school's huge library. He was a solid B student and had many friends. Although he was small, he was good at sports. He led the football team in scoring during his senior year. Joe also served as president of his senior class. In that leadership role, he gave a speech at his 1961 high school graduation.

Fast Fact

To help pay for his expensive high school, Joe Biden washed the school's windows and weeded its garden.

"He was a skinny kid, but he was one of the best pass receivers I had in 16 years as a coach."

–E. John Walsh, Biden's high school football coach

Joe Biden attended law school at Syracuse University in New York.

Dorm Days

After high school, Joe Biden attended the University of Delaware. At first, he was more interested in sports and an active social life than in studying. He learned in other ways, though. He gained debate skills by talking politics with friends. Then, in the summer of 1962, Biden was the only white lifeguard at a Wilmington pool. He learned about the struggles of being black in America from his African American friends.

By his junior year of college, Biden got serious about school. He had decided to become a lawyer and wanted to get into a good law school.

Fast Fact

In high school, politics appealed to Joe Biden. When he learned that Congress was full of lawyers, he made law school a goal.

Finding Focus

While a college junior, Biden met a young woman named Neilia Hunter. She changed his life. On weekends, he would drive more than 300 miles (483 kilometers) from Delaware to Skaneateles, New York, where she lived. She helped him focus on his schoolwork.

After he graduated from the University of Delaware in 1965, Biden attended Syracuse University College of Law. He and Neilia continued dating. He didn't always enjoy law school, but he studied hard for his exams. In 1966, at the end of his first year of law school, Joe and Neilia got married.

Fast Fact

Biden learned to water-ski to impress his then-girlfriend, Neilia Hunter.

"Get Up, Champ!"

Joseph Biden, Joe's father, faced ups and downs in his life. He joined his cousin's successful business right after high school but was forced to move on when it soured. When Joey was just a toddler, his father moved the family twice to start new businesses, each of which failed. He pushed on, though, and taught his son to never give up. "Get up, champ!" he would tell him.

A Rising Star

Biden graduated from law school in 1968. His father helped him get a job by calling a friend whose son was a judge. Biden got an interview with the best law firm in Delaware. The firm decided they would take a chance and hire him.

With Neilia, Biden moved back to Delaware, and he began his law career. But the job didn't feel right to him. He found it difficult to represent wealthy large businesses. He sympathized with the workers because of their worries about money.

Martin Luther King Jr. was a great inspiration to Biden.

Fighting For Fairness

Biden was influenced by the 1960s **civil rights** movement. Martin Luther King Jr. had fought for equal rights for African Americans. After Dr. King was killed in 1968, Biden paid close attention to the unrest that sprang up in many American cities. He decided he wanted to work to advance the cause of equal rights for all Americans. So he quit the law firm to become a **public defender**.

Ted Kennedy and Joe Biden discuss an issue in the Senate.

The Kennedy Connection

Biden listened closely to President John F. Kennedy's **inauguration** speech in 1961. He found that Kennedy's ideas about fairness and service echoed what he had been taught at home.

Biden later gained great respect for President Kennedy's brother Robert F. Kennedy, who was a civil rights activist. Another brother, Senator Ted Kennedy, had perhaps the greatest influence on Biden. Ted Kennedy became an adviser and good friend.

Fatherhood

In 1969, Biden became a father. Neilia gave birth to Joseph Robinette Biden III (called Beau). One year later, Biden's second son, Hunter, was born.

The family of four lived in a cottage at a Delaware swim club. The cottage was so small that baby Beau had to sleep in a closet. Neilia was teaching school while Joe worked as both a lawyer and a lifeguard. They hoped to save enough money to buy their dream home—especially when they learned that another baby was on the way!

Political Beginnings

Although Biden was set on being a public defender, he could get only part-time work. He also took a job at a law firm in Wilmington. He argued tough cases and learned to be a sharp lawyer.

Biden joined a group working to improve the Democratic Party in Delaware. His fresh ideas were noticed, and before long he was asked to run for office. Biden's wife and sister helped run his campaign for New Castle County Council in 1970.

Running as a Democrat in a largely Republican district was a challenge. However, Biden impressed voters by knocking on doors, meeting people face-to-face, and listening to their concerns. That strategy was successful, and he won the election.

Fast Fact

Following the county council victory, Biden's sister, Valerie, went on to manage other campaigns for her brother.

"Everything was happening faster than I expected."

–Joe Biden, speaking about his first political campaign in 1970

Full Days and Nights

As a county councilman, Biden worked to stop big corporations from harming the environment. Meanwhile, he started his own law firm.

In 1971, Biden was busy building his business and working as a local leader. His third child, Naomi, was born, and his family had a new house. He also helped search for the best Democratic candidate to represent Delaware in the U.S. Senate. The search came to a surprising end. Political leaders knocked on Biden's door and asked him to run.

Neilia Biden joins Joe and sons Beau (right) and Hunter at a reception in 1972.

A Family Affair

Biden's family joined him in his first bid for the Senate. His sister, Valerie, was in charge of his campaign. His brother, Jimmy, a college senior, helped raise money. His teenage brother, Frankie (who was born after Biden had left home), organized young volunteers. His mother helped at "coffee hours" to meet families across the state. Biden was not as well organized or well funded as his rival. But his family helped him spread his message to as many voters as possible.

The Underdog

Biden decided to go for the election. He saw it as a chance to help the people of his state. Some questioned such an inexperienced young lawyer trying to compete against J. Caleb Boggs. Boggs was a well-known senator who had also served in the U.S. **House of Representatives** and as governor of Delaware.

However, newspaper reporters began to call Biden one of the state's rising stars. Biden liked to travel with Neilia, Beau, Hunter, and Naomi in his station wagon. They toured Delaware, day after day, meeting with voters.

Fast Fact

According to the U.S. Constitution, senators have to be at least 30 years old. Biden didn't turn 30 until a few weeks after the election.

Work in Washington

The Senate race was tight. Biden's campaign spent its last few dollars on radio ads. Neilia's parents even came down from New York to support Biden—and her father was a Republican!

There was a big turnout on Election Day. Biden waited in a Wilmington hotel for the election results. It looked as if he might win, but it didn't seem real until the phone rang. Senator Boggs called to congratulate Biden on winning the election. Biden was going to the U.S. Senate!

Biden speaks to reporters in Washington, shortly after his election to the Senate.

Off to Washington

"Election Day was like a dream," Biden recalls. He was still thrilled when he went to Washington, D.C., to begin work before he officially took office. He was thinking about moving his family there and about all he wanted to tackle for the people of Delaware.

Biden entered the Senate office building as one of history's youngest senators. He felt a rush of emotion. To get started, he called on his sister to help hire a staff.

Fast Fact

Because Biden had the least experience of any senator, his first office was small and separate from most of the other senators' offices.

From Victory to Tragedy

On December 18, 1972, just a month after the election, Neilia had planned to take the three children to buy a Christmas tree. Biden was at work in Washington with his sister. Valerie took a phone call and turned pale. She and Biden rushed to a hospital in Wilmington, where they faced terrible news. Biden's wife and baby daughter had been killed in a car accident. His two sons were badly hurt.

After the loss of Neilia and Naomi, Biden devoted more time to his sons.

Biden spent weeks at the hospital, staying with Beau and Hunter until they recovered. He struggled with the deep pain of losing Neilia and Naomi. "My life had been kicked out from under me," Biden later wrote.

Sister, Best Friend

Biden's sister took on a vital role after the tragedy. Valerie quit her job and moved in to take care of Beau and Hunter. Biden recalls that she did all the shopping, cooking, and laundry.

Aunt Val played with Beau and Hunter every day and knew their needs. She helped her brother just as she had when he ran for office. She was his best friend, and Biden was forever thankful for her support. "Valerie Biden was the cornerstone that allowed me to sustain and then rebuild my family," Biden explained.

Seated in the Senate

After the accident, Biden no longer wanted to be a senator. His only concern was being a father to his sons. However, senators called him every day. They convinced him to keep his promise to represent the people of Delaware.

Fast Fact

Biden turned down many after-work invitations as a new senator to go home to his sons.

Biden didn't attend the ceremony in Washington, D.C., in which new senators were sworn in. Instead, he took his oath at the hospital. Eventually, Biden returned to work. He learned the ways of the Senate, not only through meetings but also through talking to other senators in the Senate cafeteria and the gym.

Jumping Into the Job

Once Beau and Hunter came home from the hospital, Valerie cared for them. Biden approached his Senate work more eagerly once he knew his boys were in good hands. However, he still commuted an hour and a half to be home with them each night. He also left instructions with his staff to always find him if his sons called.

Fast Fact

Biden served in the Senate for 36 years. He is the longest-serving senator in Delaware history.

Experienced senators offered him guidance. He learned to respect the other senators even if he didn't agree with their ideas. Six years passed, and Biden was ready for more. In 1978, he was reelected to the Senate. During his second term, he took on more responsibility. He worked with President Jimmy Carter and played an important role in meetings with the **Soviet Union**. He also earned spots on two important Senate committees.

"For the first time, the Senate seemed fun."

–Joe Biden, after he began dating his future wife Jill

Jill Biden

Jill Jacobs was a student at the University of Delaware when she met Joe. After they got married, she worked as a teacher and raised their family. She also earned two master's degrees: one in reading education from West Chester University in 1981 and one in English education from Villanova University in 1987. In 2007, she earned her doctorate in education from the University of Delaware. Jill has started charities to teach girls about breast cancer, to help military families, and to get books for children in low-income families.

Joe and Jill Biden share a dance at a 2009 Inauguration Day ball.

A New Beginning

Although dating was far from Biden's mind in 1975, his brother set him up with Jill Jacobs. Biden was grateful he did.

Jill was good company for Biden, and she enjoyed being with his two sons. Seven-year-old Beau soon decided it was time they—the boys and their dad—married Jill. She wasn't ready, but Biden was patient. He proposed at least five times before she said yes. In 1977, Jill and Joe got married in New York City.

Run For Number One

In the 1980s, Biden's career took off. He was known in the Senate for strong speaking skills. In fact, supporters asked him to run for president of the United States in 1980 and again in 1984. He thought that he needed more Senate experience.

Biden was figuring out which political issues mattered most to him. He worked on improving schools, keeping communities safe, and giving accused criminals fair trials. He listened to the concerns of the people in his state.

Joe Biden spends time with his daughter, Ashley.

Family First

While Biden's career thrived, his commitment to his family stayed strong. He and Jill had a daughter, Ashley, in 1981. His job took him on trips around the world, but he always made time for Beau, Hunter, and Ashley. He was at their sports games, birthday parties, and many everyday events. He had professional demands, but he never forgot his job as a father.

Fast Fact

On a typical day, Biden traveled 90 minutes each way by train between Washington, D.C., and his home in Wilmington, Delaware.

An Important Decision

By the late 1980s, Biden had his own ideas about running the country. He felt it was the right time to discuss his vision for the future. On June 9, 1987, Biden declared that he would be a candidate for the Democratic nomination for president.

Fast Fact

Unlike other political leaders, Biden has not acquired great wealth. A study found Biden to be the least wealthy of all senators in 2006.

He sprang into action, as did a number of other Democratic leaders. Among the candidates were civil rights leader Jesse Jackson, Senator Al Gore of Tennessee, and Massachusetts governor Michael Dukakis. Biden traveled around the country to meet voters and debate against his fellow candidates.

Beau Biden

When his father first ran for president, Beau was a freshman at the University of Pennsylvania. Like his father, Beau graduated from Syracuse University College of Law. He served in the U.S. Department of Justice and as a prosecutor for the U.S. government. In 2007, he became Delaware's **attorney general**. In 2008, he went to Iraq for a year in the Delaware National Guard. He returned home for a short time to see his father sworn in as vice president.

Biden shakes hands at a campaign stop in 1987.

Juggling Jobs

Running for president was no easy task. It took a vast amount of money and time for Biden to become recognized throughout the country.

Biden struggled to balance his campaign, his Senate responsibilities, and his personal life. He had promised Democratic leaders in the Senate that he would be in Washington when his vote was needed. At the time, a political battle was heating up for the Democrats in Congress.

Fast Fact

When Biden announced that he was running for president in 1987, fewer than one in five Americans knew his name.

Political Ups and Downs

Supreme Court justice Lewis Powell retired the month Biden began his presidential bid. President Ronald Reagan selected Judge Robert Bork as Powell's replacement. Biden led the committee that questioned Bork about his experience as a judge. This role meant Biden had more leadership in the Senate but less time to campaign for president.

Joe Biden speaks with Robert Bork after the first day of hearings.

Judging Judges

In 1987, Biden became chair of the Senate committee responsible for questioning potential Supreme Court justices. His job in 1987 was to research Judge Bork's courtroom decisions and question him about them. Biden called on his own law background for this role. Some people disagreed with Bork's view of the law. Biden respected Bork, and many people believed that Biden questioned him fairly. After the Senate committee voted down Bork, Anthony Kennedy became the next Supreme Court justice.

Growing Headaches

Biden was dividing his time between the Senate and his campaign. He made mistakes, and the press noticed. Biden saw that he was at a turning point. He had connected with voters. However, he thought that he wouldn't be able to both win the presidency and successfully lead the Bork hearings in the Senate. He dropped out of the race for president.

After the hearings were over, people asked Biden to talk about the experience. He was soon on the road again giving speeches. Unfortunately, he was suffering from headaches that didn't go away. After a speech in Rochester, New York, Biden had an awful night. He woke up in severe pain. He returned to Delaware, and his wife rushed him to the hospital.

Fast Fact

Biden is known for writing speeches just before giving them, sometimes on the backs of envelopes.

"There will be other presidential campaigns, and I'll be there, out front."

—Joe Biden, on withdrawing from the presidential campaign in 1987

Promises to Keep

Biden learned that he had two **aneurysms** near his brain. Doctors explained that this meant two arteries had become weak. The arteries were leaking blood. He needed surgery.

The first operation was done at a hospital in Washington, D.C., in 1988. It went well, and Biden was soon sent home. During his recovery, however, he developed a blood clot in his lung. Clots are lumps that can block the flow of blood. After a second surgery, he was home again, at last.

Biden makes his first public appearance following his surgeries in 1988.

Back on Track

Seven months later, on September 7, 1988, Biden was feeling better. He boarded an Amtrak train in Wilmington. His wife, children, parents, and siblings all escorted him to Washington for his first day back in the Senate.

Like his father had taught him, Biden got back up. He kept his promise to serve his country and the people of his state. He knew, though, that he couldn't keep working at such a fast pace.

Fast Fact

Biden gives names to the houses he lives in, including "The Station," "North Star," and "The Lake House," all homes in the Wilmington area.

Biden works on international and security issues with President Bill Clinton (center) in 1997.

Thinking Globally

After his recovery, Biden remained committed to his work in the Senate. **Foreign relations** had been important to Biden since the 1970s. He consulted with European, Middle Eastern, and Asian leaders since early in his career. He went on to lead the Senate committee in charge of foreign relations.

Biden became a strong leader on foreign policy. He spoke out against President Ronald Reagan's foreign policies in the 1980s. He disapproved of President George H. W. Bush's plan for the Gulf War in Iraq in 1991. Biden has supported military action in some cases, however, including a conflict in southeastern Europe in the late 1990s. Biden was a key adviser to President Bill Clinton at the time.

Fast Fact

Biden published his memoir, *Promises to Keep*, in 2007. It became a best seller after he was picked to run for vice president.

Acting Locally

While Biden worked for **diplomacy** abroad, he remembered everyday Americans at home. Beginning in 1990, he proposed laws to protect women against violence at home, at school, and at work. He found unexpected resistance from his fellow senators. But Biden didn't give up. He believed strongly in his efforts to help protect women.

Eventually, he succeeded in adding more rights for women into an anticrime law being voted on by the Senate. Known as the Violence Against Women Act, it was signed into law by President Clinton in 2000. Biden says this bill is "what I'm most proud of in my entire career."

> "Let us roll up our sleeves to roll back this awful tide of violence and reduce crime in our country."
>
> —President Bill Clinton, after signing a law that included the Violence Against Women Act

Reliving History

Biden's knowledge of the Middle East became critical after the terrorist attacks on the United States on September 11, 2001. He consulted with President George W. Bush but didn't agree with all of the president's plans for military action in Afghanistan and Iraq. By 2004, he believed America needed someone new in the White House.

Fast Fact

The Bidens spend every Thanksgiving on Nantucket, an island off the coast of Massachusetts.

Biden had high hopes for his friend, Senator John Kerry, in the 2004 presidential election. However, George W. Bush defeated Kerry. Looking toward the next election, Biden decided he would again run for president. His short candidacy in 1987 had been hard on his family, but they supported his bid for president in 2008.

> "We think you're the best person to pull the country together."
>
> —Jill Biden, supporting her husband's 2008 run for the presidency

Mom Mom

Biden's mother supported him all his life. Jean, or "Mom Mom" to Biden, taught him the values he carried with him from his home in Scranton to the U.S. Senate. She helped him work on his stutter as a child. She also taught him that he was no better than anyone else, regardless of his job or how well he was dressed. At 92 years old, Jean saw her son take the oath as vice president of the United States on January 20, 2009.

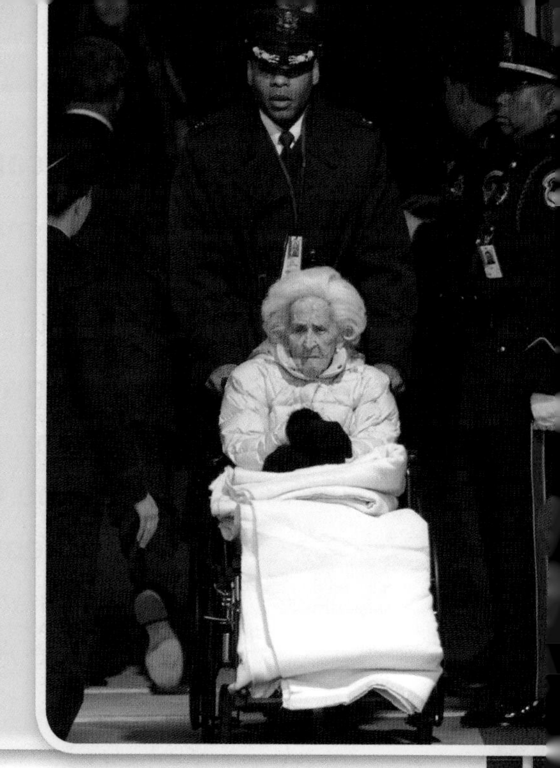

A New Role

It turned out that 2008 was not Biden's year to become president. Senators Hillary Clinton and Barack Obama became the Democratic Party's front-runners. But Biden was not overlooked. He was a candidate who understood the values of working people and had strong foreign policy experience.

Obama had captured the hearts of many American voters. When he became the Democratic candidate, he sought someone with solid experience to be his running mate. He chose Joe Biden.

Fast Fact

Jill promised her husband a dog if he and Obama won the 2008 election. Biden picked a German shepherd puppy. His grandchildren named it Champ.

The American Dream

At the Democratic **National Convention** in Denver, Colorado, in August 2008, Biden told his life story. "I'm here for everyone I grew up with in Scranton and Wilmington," he said. "I'm here for the cops and the firefighters, the teachers and the assembly line workers, the folks whose lives are the very measure of whether the American dream endures."

Biden and Obama wave to the crowd at the Democratic National Convention in August 2008.

Republican vice presidential candidate Sarah Palin shakes hands with Biden after their debate in 2008.

The Running Mate

As Barack Obama's running mate, Biden campaigned throughout the fall of 2008. He debated the Republican vice presidential candidate, Governor Sarah Palin of Alaska. He traveled all over the country, talking to voters about the economy and other issues.

On Election Day 2008, more Americans went to the voting booths than ever before. With the help of Pennsylvania and other key states, Obama and Biden won. It was a commanding victory for the Democratic ticket.

Fast Fact

The Biden-Palin debate on October 2, 2008, was the most-watched vice presidential debate of all time.

Mr. Vice President

Obama promised Biden a partnership, with weekly meetings for the two to share their ideas. Even before Biden took office, he traveled to Asia and Iraq to help plan U.S. policy there. He laid the groundwork for leading the Middle Class Task Force. This new group's goal is to help working- and middle-class families.

Fast Fact

The U.S. Secret Service code name for Biden is "Celtic," which refers to his Irish background.

Civil rights first drove Biden to the Senate. So it was fitting that he was sworn in next to the nation's first African American president. On January 20, 2009, he joined Barack Obama on the steps of the Capitol in Washington, D.C. The two men took their oaths before a record crowd. More than 1 million people stood in the cold at the National Mall and along the parade route.

"Washington hasn't changed him. Instead, Joe Biden has changed Washington."

–Barack Obama, at the Wilmington train station on his way to the inauguration

---

The Bidens join Barack and Michelle Obama before an inauguration concert on the National Mall.

Getting to Work

On Inauguration Day, Biden placed his hand on the huge family Bible he brought with him. In his strong voice, he promised to uphold his duties as the 47th vice president of the United States. His family congratulated him, and the crowd cheered. Then, like he had done all his life, he got right to work.

Time Line

1942	Joseph Robinette Biden Jr. is born on November 20 in Scranton, Pennsylvania.
1965	Biden graduates from the University of Delaware with a degree in history and political science.
1966	Biden marries Neilia Hunter.
1968	Biden graduates from Syracuse University College of Law and begins work as a lawyer.
1972	Biden is elected a U.S. senator from Delaware. His wife and daughter are killed in a car accident.
1977	Biden marries Jill Jacobs.
1987	Biden announces his candidacy for president. He announces a second run in 2007.
2008	Biden is chosen as Barack Obama's running mate on the Democratic ticket.
2009	Biden is sworn in as vice president of the United States on January 20.

Glossary

aneurysms: swellings in a weakened part of arteries, caused by disease or injury

attorney general: the top law officer of a state or country

blue-collar: relating to people who do manual labor and get paid hourly

campaign: a race between candidates for an office or position

candidate: a person who is running for office

civil rights: rights of citizens to political and social equality and freedom

debate: contest in which two sides argue opposing points of view

diplomacy: negotiations between different groups

foreign relations: the dealings or connections between the United States and other countries

House of Representatives: a house of the U.S. Congress, with 435 voting members elected to two-year terms.

inauguration: a ceremony in which a person takes office

national convention: a large gathering of a political party, at which a candidate for president is officially announced

public defender: a government lawyer who provides free defense to people accused of crimes

senator: one of the 100 voting members in the house of the U.S. Congress called the Senate. Senators are elected to six-year terms.

Soviet Union: a country that existed from 1922 to 1991. In 1991, it was broken up into Russia and other 15 countries.

Find Out More

Books

Brown, Jonathan A. *Delaware* (Portraits of the States). Milwaukee, WI: Gareth Stevens, 2007.

Goodman, Susan E. *See How They Run: Campaign Dreams, Election Schemes, and the Race to the White House*. New York: Bloombury, 2008.

Horn, Geoffrey M. *Barack Obama* (People We Should Know). Pleasantville, NY: Gareth Stevens, 2009.

Thomas, William David. *How Do We Elect Our Leaders?* (My American Government). Pleasantville, NY: Gareth Stevens, 2008.

Travis, Cathy. *Constitution Translated for Kids*. 3rd ed. Austin, TX: Synergy Books, 2006.

Web Sites

Ben's Guide to U.S. Government for Kids
http://bensguide.gpo.gov
Find out how the U.S. government works and how the president and vice president are elected.

Congress for Kids
www.congressforkids.net
This site offers information about the U.S. Congress, where Joe Biden served for 36 years.

The White House
www.whitehouse.gov
Learn about the history of the White House, find out about current news, and read biographies of Vice President Biden and other people in office.

Source Notes

p. 5: "Biden Talks Politics Back Home in Scranton," ABC News blog, September 1, 2008, www.blogs.abcnews.com/politicalradar/2008/09/biden-talks-pol.html.

p. 8: John L. Micek, "Clintons Join Biden on Familiar Turf," *Los Angeles Times*, October 13, 2008.

p. 9: Kenneth P. Vogel and Alexander Burns, "Sen. Joe Biden (D-Scranton)," *Politico*, August 28, 2008, www.politico.com/news/stories/0808/12955.html.

pp. 13, 19, 23, 24, 25, 26, 38: Joe Biden, *Promises to Keep: On Life and Politics* (New York: Random House, 2007).

p. 13 bottom: John M. Broder, "Father's Tough Life an Inspiration for Biden," *New York Times*, October 23, 2008, www.nytimes.com/2008/10/24/us/politics/24biden.html.

p. 33: E. J. Dionne Jr., "Biden Withdraws From Bid for President in Wake of Furor," *New York Times*, September 24, 1987.

p. 40: "Joseph R. Biden's Convention Speech." *New York Times*, August 27, 2008, www.nytimes.com/2008/08/27/us/politics/27text-biden.html?_r=1&oref=slogin&pagewanted=all.

p. 42: "Obama in Delaware," prepared text of Barack Obama's remarks, New York Times, January 17, 2009, www.nytimes.com/2009/01/17/us/politics/17text-obama-delaware.html?ref=politics.

Index

About the Author

Nicole Iorio has been writing for children for a decade. She also writes and edits lessons for teachers. She lives in New Jersey with her husband and two sons. She dedicates this book to Marlowe and Colin, who were enthralled by the 2008 election and witnessed the historic inauguration, even spotting Joe Biden as he marched in the parade.